A TASTE OF ITALY

Jenny Ridgwell

Thomson Learning

New York

Titles in this series

A TASTE OF

Italy

Japan

Cover *Sunflowers growing in front of a hilltop village in Tuscany, northern Italy.*

Frontispiece *Sweet red peppers were brought to Italy from Central and South America in the sixteenth century. They are now an important ingredient in Italian cooking.*

First published in the
United States in 1993 by
Thomson Learning
115 Fifth Avenue
New York, NY 10003

First published in 1993 by
Wayland (Publishers) Ltd.

Library of Congress Cataloging-in-Publication Data
Ridgwell, Jenny.
A taste of Italy / Jenny Ridgwell.
p. cm. (Food around the world)
Includes bibliographical references and index.
Summary: Provides an overview of Italian cuisine and food customs,
giving some historical background as well as a variety of recipes with a
glossary of pertinent terms appended.
ISBN 1-56847-098-3 : $14.95
[1. Cookery, Italian —Juvenile literature. 2. Food habits—Italy.
3. Italy—Social life and customs.] I. Title. II. Series.
TX723.R49   1993
641.59454—dc20   93-25200

Printed in Italy

Contents

Italy – its farming and food   4

Italian food in the past   8

The Italian way of life   12

Pasta   16

Meat and fish   20

Cheese   22

Other important ingredients   24

Drinks   28

Festival food   30

Minestrone   32

Bean and tuna fish salad   34

Pasta with ham and leek   36

Risotto with sausage   38

Granita di limone   40

Neapolitan pizza   42

Glossary   45

Books to Read   47

Index   48

Italy – its farming and food

Above *Rome is a busy, crowded city.*
Below *Grapevines in northern Italy, with mountains in the background. Much of Italy is mountainous.*

Italy is a long, narrow country sticking out from Europe into the Mediterranean Sea. It is 750 miles long from north to south. In shape, it looks sort of like a boot. In the north, Italy is separated from the rest of Europe by the high mountains of the Alps. Two large Mediterranean islands, Sicily and Sardinia, are also part of Italy.

Italy is one of the most crowded countries in Europe. It has a population of about 58 million people, most of whom live in the cities and towns. Rome is the capital city.

Farming

In the past many Italians were farmers. Over the last 50 years, however, Italian industry has grown quickly. Nowadays, more people work in industry than in farming.

Much of the land is mountainous, which makes farming difficult in these areas. However, Italy still manages to produce a lot of food. The main crops are grapes, wheat, and olives.

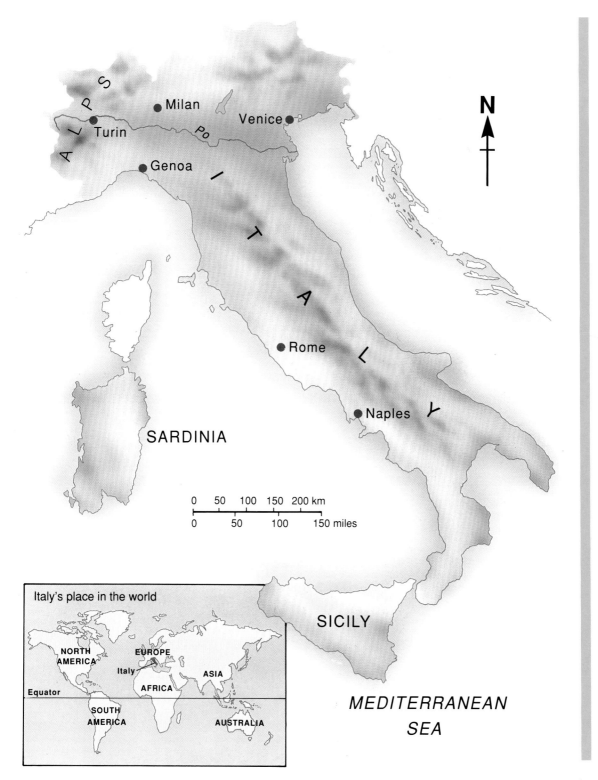

N

ALPS

Milan

Turin

Venice

Po

Genoa

ITALY

Rome

Naples

SARDINIA

0   50   100   150 200 km

0   50   100   150 miles

Italy's place in the world

NORTH
AMERICA

EUROPE

Italy

ASIA

AFRICA

Equator

SOUTH
AMERICA

AUSTRALIA

SICILY

MEDITERRANEAN
SEA

A taste of Italy

Wheat and grapes are important crops. This picture shows rolling wheat fields as well as vines.

The hills of southern Italy are covered with groves of olive trees.

Italy is famous for its wine (made from grapes) and is the second largest producer of olive oil in the world. It is also the second largest wheat producer in Europe. Two types of wheat are grown: hard wheat for making pasta and soft wheat for making bread.

Other important crops include rice, corn, and citrus fruits such as lemons and oranges.

Cattle, sheep, and goats are raised for their meat and for milk. Milk is used to make butter and cheese. Pigs are also important, because Italy produces a lot of ham and salami, made from pork.

Climate

Because of Italy's long shape, there is a big difference in climate between northern and southern areas. This has an effect on the farming and cooking in the different regions.

In the cooler north of Italy there is rich farmland for growing cereal crops. The north also has plenty of grazing land for cattle, which are used to produce milk. People in the north use a lot of butter, cheese, and milk in their cooking.

In the hot south there are many olive groves and vineyards. People also grow salad vegetables, such as tomatoes and peppers. In southern regions, people use olive oil instead of butter for cooking and they eat delicious salads.

The mountains of northern Italy provide grazing for cattle.

Peppers, onions, and tomatoes are important ingredients in southern Italy.

Italian food in the past

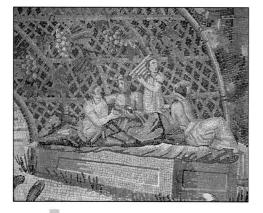

The ancient Romans enjoyed lavish feasts. They lay down on long benches to eat and were served by slaves.

Food in Roman times

Over 2,000 years ago the ancient Romans ruled Italy. It seems that they were very good cooks. Many of today's Italian foods, such as wild boar and songbirds, can be traced back to Roman times. Rich people ate huge amounts of expensive foods. Writers from Roman times tell of tables laden with cooked peacocks, flamingos, and herons. Dormice were another favorite Roman food. The dormice were kept and fattened up in special barrels.

Songbirds are still a popular food in Italy. This dish of roast thrush comes from Sardinia.

The Romans divided their large meals into three parts. This habit was copied by other Europeans and still exists. The antipasto course was eaten first to make the eater feel hungry. Antipasto is Italian for "before the meal." The main part of the meal was meat, fish, and vegetables. Finally, there was a dish of sweet foods, such as grapes and dates.

The Romans learned how to make salt from seawater. Salt is a very important ingredient. It is useful for seasoning and preserving food. The Romans became wealthy from selling salt to other parts of the world.

It must be remembered, however, that most ordinary Romans ate quite a poor diet. A meal was often thick porridge followed by coarse bread with olives, beans, figs, and cheese.

The Middle Ages

During the Middle Ages, Arabs from northern Africa settled in southern Italy and Sicily. They brought with them the art of making sweets from honey and nuts.

Spices from Asia were also introduced and imported through Genoa and Venice. Italians learned to use these new spices in their cooking. Saffron, for example, was and still is used in risotto.

Risotto made with saffron. The saffron gives the rice a bright yellow color.

A taste of Italy

Above *Hot peppers are dried in the air.* Below *Italian plum tomatoes are long and thin, not round.*

Foods from the Americas

In the fifteenth century European explorers reached the Americas for the first time. Over the years, sailors brought back foods from North and South America that had never been seen in Europe. These included tomatoes, potatoes, corn, and sweet peppers.

The first tomatoes brought to Italy from South America were yellow. Later, however, people discovered that red tomatoes grew well in the warm Italian climate. Today, both fresh and canned Italian tomatoes are sold to many parts of the world.

Potatoes were brought from Peru. At first they were grown in Italian gardens as decorative plants. Later, people discovered they were good to eat, too.

Corn was first brought to Italy in about 1650. It was made into a thick, yellow porridge, called polenta. Polenta soon became a popular food in Italy. It is still served today, with meat stews or mixed with butter and cheese.

Polenta, made from cornmeal, is often served with stews.

Italian food around the world

Over the years, many people from the southern regions of Italy have left to live in other countries, such as the United States, Canada, and Australia. These settlers have often set up Italian grocery stores and restaurants in their new countries. Today, Italian food is popular in many countries of the world.

The Italian way of life

Italians love to sit in cafes and chat with friends over a cup of coffee.

Family, friends, and food play an important part in Italian life. Families meet regularly for meals and celebrations. In many towns people go for an evening stroll around the streets, and friends gather for coffee and ice cream in cafes and at counters.

Everyday eating

Italians eat bread with every meal. In many families, the first job of the day is to go out to a bakery to buy some fresh bread.

Breakfast is usually a quick snack of milky coffee or hot drinking chocolate, with sweet rolls or croissants.

Bread stalls sell fresh bread every day.

Many Italians have a long lunch break of about two hours. Stores and offices close and families often go home to eat. Some schoolchildren may take a packed lunch from home if their school is a long way away.

The main meal of the day is in the evening and is eaten at about 7 P.M. It might consist of vegetable soup, bread, meat, and salad, followed by fruit.

Lunch is a time for the whole family to get together for a meal.

13

Shopping

In general, Italians like to buy fresh food each day from small local shops. As a result, Italy has more small grocery stores than any other country in Europe. In recent years, large supermarkets have opened on the outskirts of towns and cities. However, compared to other countries, these are few in number.

Most towns have a special market day once a week, when stalls are set up in a square in the town center. These markets are always busy places, with stalls selling fresh fruit, vegetables, cheeses, and meat.

Above *Italians tend to prefer shopping at small grocery stores rather than at supermarkets.*

Market day in Padua, a large city in northern Italy.

Cooking

Italians like to eat good quality food prepared using traditional methods. Italian cooks tend to use simple, basic equipment rather than modern machines and gadgets.

For example, only 4 percent of the homes in Italy have a microwave oven. In the United States the figure is 61 percent. Only 28 percent of Italian homes have a freezer, compared with 87 percent in Norway and Sweden.

How healthy is the Italian diet?

Scientists have studied what they call the "Mediterranean diet." This is the type of food generally eaten by people in the Mediterranean region – including the Italians. The Mediterranean diet consists of plenty of starchy foods, such as bread, pasta, and potatoes, lots of fresh fruit and vegetables, olive oil, and fish – and a little wine sometimes!

Scientists have discovered that people who eat a Mediterranean diet are less likely to suffer from heart disease. They also do not suffer greatly from food-related illnesses such as constipation and diabetes. Food experts suggest that people should copy this way of eating in order to stay healthy.

This chart shows the different types of food eaten, per person, in Italy and the United States each year.

You can see that the Italians eat much more starchy food, such as flour and potatoes, and get less fat from milk than people in the United States. They eat less sugar too.

	Italy lbs.	United States lbs.
flour	254	185
potatoes	310	127
meat	196	112
milk	165	571
butter	4.4	4.4
sugar	4.4	64

Pasta

Twists, tubes, shells, and bows – these are just some of the hundreds of different shapes of pasta.

There are hundreds of different shapes of pasta – and hundreds of different names for the shapes! Italian pasta dishes have become popular all over the world.

No one knows when the Italians started to eat pasta. One popular story is that the Italian explorer Marco Polo, who traveled to Asia in the thirteenth century, brought back the recipe from China. In China people eat egg noodles, which are similar to pasta. It seems, though, that people in Europe have been eating some form of pasta for several thousand years.

The word "pasta" means paste or dough in Italian. Pasta is made from a special hard wheat, called durum wheat, which is mixed with water, and sometimes milk or eggs, to form a dough.

Over the years the Italians have invented many different shapes and sizes of pasta. Shapes are made by pressing the dough into molds to make shells or spirals, or by squeezing it out to make lengths for vermicelli, macaroni, or spaghetti.

Pasta is made from very simple ingredients – flour, water, and sometimes eggs.

Many Italians use pasta machines. The dough is put in at the back of the machine and is squeezed out through metal "teeth" to make flat noodles, spaghetti, or macaroni.

A taste of Italy

The pasta can be used fresh, or it can be dried and kept for later. Either way, it is cooked by boiling it in water for several minutes until it is soft but chewy.

Pasta can be made in different colors and flavors by adding other ingredients. For example, green spinach, red tomatoes, or black squid ink can be mixed into the dough. People have even made chocolate-flavored pasta!

Red, black, green, and brown pasta.

Make your own pasta

In Italy people use special machines to make pasta at home. The dough is squeezed through holes to make thin, flat noodles or round lengths of spaghetti or macaroni. This is an easy recipe for making pasta by hand.

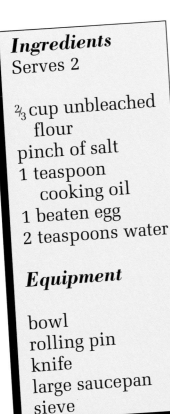

Ingredients
Serves 2

$\frac{2}{3}$ cup unbleached
　flour
pinch of salt
1 teaspoon
　cooking oil
1 beaten egg
2 teaspoons water

Equipment

bowl
rolling pin
knife
large saucepan
sieve

1　Put all the ingredients in a bowl and mix with your hands to make a dough. Squeeze and knead it for 2-3 minutes until it is smooth.

18

2   Sprinkle some flour onto a work top and roll out the dough very thin.

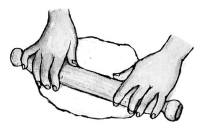

3   Cut it into strips or invent your own shapes.

4   Cook for 3-5 minutes in a large saucepan of boiling water. The pasta should be soft but still firm and chewy.

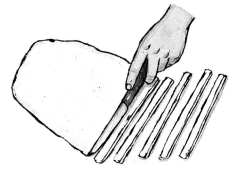

5   Drain through a sieve over the sink. Serve hot with tomato sauce or *pesto* (basil and garlic sauce). You can buy ready-made sauces in jars from supermarkets.

Always be careful with boiling water. Ask an adult to help you.

A simple dish of pasta with pesto *sauce.*

Meat and fish

Meat, poultry, and game

Besides the usual animals raised for meat – beef cattle, sheep, pigs, and chickens – Italians also enjoy eating animals caught for sport. This meat is called game, and includes rabbit, wild boar, and small birds.

Italy is famous for some of its meat products, such as hams and sausages.

Parma ham is a dark red color.

Parma ham

Ham is made from the back leg of a pig, which is treated with salt. This process is called "curing." In years gone by, curing was a way of preserving the meat to make it last through the winter.

Parma ham is the best-known Italian ham. It is cured, then left for a year before it is eaten. This long process makes Parma ham expensive to buy. It is cut into very thin slices and people eat only a little at a time!

Salami

Salami is a kind of spicy sausage that was invented in Italy. Now, however, many other countries have copied the recipe. Salami is made from chopped meat mixed with salt and spices, such as pepper, paprika, and garlic. The sausage is then dried in the air or smoked.

Many different types of salami are made in Italy.

Fish and seafood are best eaten very fresh. These harborside stalls sell fish straight from the fishing boats.

Fish

Italians eat a huge variety of sea fish, such as tuna fish, hake, sardines, and anchovies. They also eat other seafood, such as lobsters, shrimp, mussels, squid, and octopus, and freshwater fish, including trout.

Fishing is an important industry in Italy, particularly in Sicily and Sardinia. However, over the years the Mediterranean has become more and more polluted. Now the fishing boats travel farther for their catches – even as far as the Atlantic Ocean.

21

Cheese

The ancient Romans made at least thirteen different cheeses. Some of their recipes are still used today. The Italians make cheese out of milk from cows, sheep, goats, and even buffalo.

Parmesan

Parmesan (or *Parmegiano reggiano*) is the cheese grated over pasta. It is made in northern Italy. As much as 35 pounds (about 4.5 gallons) of skim milk is used to make 2 pounds of cheese. The cheese is then left for two years. Parmesan is hard and salty. It will keep for several years.

Above *The Italians produce a wide variety of hard and soft cheeses.*
Right *Buffalo are raised for their milk, which is used to make mozzarella.*

Mozzarella
Soft, white mozzarella is the cheese used as a pizza topping. When cooked, it stretches into long strands. The best mozzarella is made from buffalo milk. Today, however, Italy has few buffalo, so cows' milk is used instead. Fresh mozzarella is kept in whey and should be eaten soon after it is made.

Gorgonzola
The famous blue cheese, Gorgonzola, comes from the north of Italy. It has a strong smell and tangy taste. To make Gorgonzola, copper wires are inserted into the cheese. This helps the mold that produces the blue color to grow.

Mozzarella and tomato salad is a delicious Italian starter.

Other important ingredients

Olives

Olives are eaten as a snack or made into olive oil.

Olives are an important crop in central and southern Italy, where olive trees grow all over the hillsides. In the autumn, when the olives are ready for picking, farmers place nets under the trees and knock off the olives with sticks. Green olives are ones that have been picked before they have ripened. Black olives have been allowed to ripen fully before picking.

At harvest time, farmers spread nets under their olive trees to catch the falling fruit.

Both black and green olives are too bitter to be eaten straight from the tree. They have to be soaked in salt water before they are ready to eat.

Whole olives, pits and all, are crushed to make olive oil. Oil from the first pressing is called "extra virgin." It is strong-tasting and expensive. The olives are then pressed again several times to produce cheaper, milder oils.

Olives change from green to black as they ripen.

Rice

Rice is the main ingredient in risotto, a dish from northern Italy. A special, very expensive rice called Arborio is used. When cooked, this rice becomes creamy on the outside, while staying crunchy in the middle.

Arborio rice is grown in the valley of the Po River. Rice needs plenty of water and warmth to grow, so the land is flooded. It then has to be drained so the rice can be harvested.

Rice fields are flooded with water before the rice seedlings are planted.

A taste of Italy

Bread is made in different shapes and flavors. Nuts and seeds are often added.

Wild mushrooms are a favorite food. Many different varieties are eaten.

Bread

The ancient Romans ate a range of different breads, both sweet and savory. To the basic flour dough, they added other ingredients, such as honey, oil, wine, and milk. The Romans ate their bread with meat or dipped it into goats' milk or wine as a quick snack.

Today, Italians eat delicious fresh bread with nearly every meal. Bread is made with white or whole-wheat flour, and there are many varieties and shapes from different regions. *Pagnotta* is a large, coarse country loaf, which keeps fresh for several days. *Panini* are long, soft rolls used for sandwiches.

Vegetables and fruit

Tomatoes, peppers, onions, and garlic are used in many Italian dishes. Fresh herbs, such as basil, oregano, and parsley, are important seasonings. Other popular vegetables in Italy include artichokes,

Other important ingredients

Sicily has an excellent climate for growing fruit and vegetables. This stall is in the Sicilian capital, Palermo.

eggplant, and spinach. The Italians also like all kinds of mushrooms.

Fruit is eaten at the end of a meal. The warm Italian climate is perfect for growing fruit such as grapes, peaches, and figs.

Ice cream and water ices

The ancient Romans discovered how to keep ice, even in summer, and made ices from frozen, sweetened water. They thought of freezing cream, too, sweetened with honey or sugar. Today, Italy is famous for its delicious ice creams.

There are two types of Italian ices. *Gelato* is made from cream and comes in flavors such as pistachio (a kind of nut), chocolate, and vanilla. *Granita* is a water ice flavored with crushed fruits, such as strawberries or lemons.

Cassata (a mixture of ice cream and fruit) and Neapolitan (layers of different ice creams) are famous Italian desserts.

Italian ice creams are often exciting mixtures of ice cream, cream, fruit, nuts, and wafers.

Drinks

Grapes are harvested in the late summer.

Wine

The Italians produce a great deal of wine. Grapes are grown in large vineyards. Often, groups of farmers from one area take their grapes to a central organization where the grapes are pressed and made into wine. Money made from selling the wine is shared among the farmers.

There are hundreds of different types of bottled wine in Italy. Famous Italian wines include Chianti (a red wine) and Asti spumante (a sweet, sparkling wine).

A modern winery. Farmers from the surrounding area bring their grapes to be pressed and made into wine.

An Italian store selling a wide range of wines and vermouths.

Italian wines are sometimes made into vermouth. This is made from wine flavored with herbs. It is drunk before lunch or dinner.

Italians drink "bitters" to soothe an upset stomach or indigestion. This is made from wine flavored with herbs and flowers – and it tastes very bitter indeed!

Coffee

Coffee was introduced into Italy from Arabia, in the Middle East, many centuries ago. The first coffee shops opened in Venice. Now they are found all around the world.

Italians drink coffee throughout the day. Cappuccino is frothy, milky coffee topped with chocolate powder and it is drunk in the morning. Strong, black espresso coffee is popular after a meal.

Cappuccino coffee is made with hot, frothy milk.

Festival food

Most Italians are Roman Catholics. Throughout the year there are many festivals linked to religious events, such as Christmas and Easter. At these times, families celebrate with special foods.

Christmas

Christmas is the most important family festival in Italy. Some Italians eat their celebration meal on Christmas Eve (December 24) before they go to church for midnight Mass. Others have their Christmas meal on Christmas Day (December 25). The meal often lasts all day!

An Italian Christmas meal is made up of many courses. In each region of Italy, different favorite specialities are included. It is followed by Italian Christmas cake, called panettone. This is a light sponge cake made from candied fruit and raisins. It is served with sweet, sparkling Asti spumante wine.

Italian Christmas cake, panettone, is a light sponge with dried fruit.

Below is an example of the kind of Christmas Eve meal that might be eaten by a family from Naples, in southern Italy.

- Rich soup made with spinach
- Pasta served with a meat and tomato sauce
- Several fish dishes, including cod and eels
- Panettone
- Nuts and fruit

- Sliced raw vegetables and mayonnaise
- Ravioli (pasta squares filled with cheese and spinach)
- Roast beef with zucchini, carrots, and fried potatoes
- Goats'-milk cheese
- Fruit and nuts
- Crème caramel
- Panettone (after a short rest!)

Above is an example of a family meal for Christmas Day in Turin, in the north of Italy.

Easter

Easter is another important festival. Most Italians eat roast lamb at Easter. In the south people make a savory round pastry with eggs and ham. In Liguria, in northwest Italy, people make an Easter pie from 33 thin sheets of pastry filled with cheese, eggs, and spinach. Each sheet of pastry stands for a year in the life of Jesus Christ.

Torrone, which is like nougat, is a traditional candy eaten as a treat at all Italian festivals.

A bakery selling special Easter breads. "Buona Pasqua" is Italian for "Happy Easter."

31

Minestrone

*Minestrone can be
made using all kinds
of vegetables –
whatever is available.*

Minestrone is a filling soup made from lots of vegetables, often with beans, and pasta. Eat it with lots of crusty bread and it is a meal in itself!

1   Heat the carrot, celery, onion, and bacon in the oil in a large saucepan. Stir all the time until the vegetables begin to soften.

Equipment

large saucepan
knife and
     chopping board
4 soup bowls
ladle

2   Pour in the water, bring to a boil, and season with salt and pepper. Then add the spaghetti, broken into small pieces. Cook for 10 minutes.

3   Add the frozen peas and cook for a further 5 minutes.

4   Ladle into large soup bowls and sprinkle on some Parmesan cheese.

Always be careful with boiling water and knives. Ask an adult to help you.

Bean and tuna fish salad

This dish is quick to make and can be eaten at the start of a meal or as a main course with other salads.

Fishing for tuna near Sicily. Tuna are very large fish. Their meaty flesh is cut into steaks.

Ingredients
Serves 2–4

1-lb. can cannellini (white kidney beans)
1 can tuna fish in water, 6⅛-oz. size
2 scallions, chopped fine
black pepper
olive oil
juice of ½ lemon

Equipment

can-opener
sieve
large bowl
knife and chopping board

1 Open the cans of beans and tuna fish. Drain off the liquid.

2 In a bowl, mix together the beans, tuna fish, and scallions. Season with pepper, a little olive oil, and lemon juice.

Always be careful with knives and can-openers. Ask an adult to help you.

3 Serve with lots of crusty bread.

The Italians eat all kinds of beans. Dried beans have to be soaked and cooked before eating. Canned beans are ready to eat.

Pasta with ham and leek

Ingredients
Serves 2

1 leek
2 tablespoons
   vegetable oil
3-4 oz. cooked ham,
   cut into thin strips
1 cup dried pasta
   spirals
$\frac{2}{3}$ cup light cream
black pepper
grated Parmesan
   cheese

Equipment

knife, chopping board
saucepan with lid
large pot
sieve
wooden spoon
paper towels
pot holders

1   Wash the leek well under running water to remove any soil, and pat dry with a paper towel. Cut it into thin slices.

2   Heat the oil in a saucepan, add the sliced leek and cook gently until it softens. Turn off the heat. Add the ham and cover with a lid.

Pasta with a cream and ham sauce is a popular dish from northern Italy.

3 Cook the pasta in a large pot of boiling water, following the instructions on the package. It should be soft but still chewy. Drain in a sieve over a sink.

4 Stir the cream into the leeks and ham and season with pepper.

Always be careful with boiling water. Ask an adult to help you.

5 Mix this sauce into the pasta and serve hot, sprinkled with Parmesan cheese.

37

Risotto with sausage

Ingredients
Serves 4

¼-½ lb. skinless
    sausages
1 onion, chopped
    fine
2 tablespoons butter
    or oil
1 cup Arborio or any
    long grain rice
2 cups water
¼ lb. mushrooms,
    sliced
2 large tomatoes,
    chopped
salt and pepper
grated Parmesan
    cheese

*All kinds of
ingredients can be
added to risotto.
This one is made
with asparagus.*

Risotto is a creamy rice dish that comes
from the north of Italy. Usually it is
made with lots of butter. For this recipe
you can use vegetable oil instead.

Equipment

knife and chopping board
saucepan with lid
heavy saucepan
wooden spoon
measuring cup
teakettle

1 Cut the sausages into slices and "dry fry" in a saucepan without any oil, stirring all the time. Add the mushrooms, tomatoes, and a little water to make a sauce. Season with salt and pepper, cover with a lid, and cook for 10 minutes.

2 Cook the onion in the butter in a heavy saucepan until soft. Add the rice and cook, stirring, for 1 minute.

3 In the teakettle bring 2 cups of water to a boil. Carefully add a little at a time to the rice, making sure all the water is absorbed. Keep stirring as it cooks. Let the rice simmer for about 10 minutes until it is soft. Add more water if needed.

> Always be careful with boiling water. Ask an adult to help you.

4 When the rice is cooked, stir in the sausage mixture and serve hot, sprinkled with grated Parmesan cheese.

Granita di limone

Italians are famous for their water ices and ice creams. Try this homemade recipe for lemon water ice. Remember to stir the mixture often as it freezes, so that the water ice is soft, not solid.

Try making orange, coffee, and strawberry water ices.

Ingredients
Serves 6

2 cups water
⅔ cup sugar
juice and rind of
2 lemons

Equipment

saucepan
grater or zester
lemon squeezer
plastic tray or bowl

1 Boil the water and sugar in a saucepan for 5 minutes, stirring to make sure the sugar dissolves.

> Always be careful with boiling water. Ask an adult to help you.

2 Remove from the heat, add the lemon juice and grated lemon rind, and leave to cool.

3 Pour into a tray or bowl that can be put in a freezer. Place in the freezer for 3-4 hours.

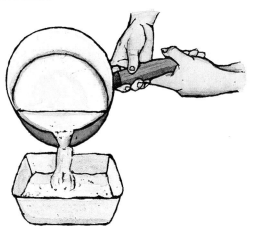

4 Stir every 30 minutes to scrape the ice crystals into the mixture. This makes a softer, finer water ice.

5 Try making other water ices flavored with orange juice, coffee, or strawberries.

Neapolitan pizza

Pizza topped with onions and red and green peppers.

The ancient Romans made a kind of pizza from bread dough, onions, and oil. There was no tomato topping because tomatoes arrived in Italy only in the fifteenth century.

Pizza is now made all over the world, but it first came from Naples. It was simply bread dough topped with tomatoes and mozzarella cheese, baked in a hot oven.

Italian families visit a pizzeria to buy pizza ready made. This idea has been copied elsewhere. Takeout pizza restaurants can now be found all over the world.

Equipment

baking sheet
measuring cup
mixing bowl
knife
rolling pin
grater
can-opener
oven mitts

Make your own pizza following this traditional recipe and add your own extra toppings.

This pizza is about to be put into the oven at an Italian pizzeria.

1 Set the oven at 425°F. Grease a large baking sheet with a little vegetable oil.

2 Make the dough. Sprinkle the yeast and sugar into the warm water in a measuring cup and leave to froth for about 10 minutes.

3 Put the flour and salt into a bowl, stir in the yeast mixture, then work into a ball with your hands.

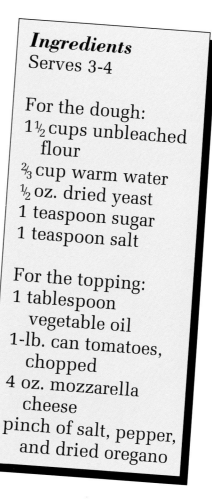

Ingredients
Serves 3-4

For the dough:
1½ cups unbleached flour
⅔ cup warm water
½ oz. dried yeast
1 teaspoon sugar
1 teaspoon salt

For the topping:
1 tablespoon vegetable oil
1-lb. can tomatoes, chopped
4 oz. mozzarella cheese
pinch of salt, pepper, and dried oregano

A taste of Italy

5 Drain the juice from the tomatoes and grate the mozzarella cheese. Brush the top of the pizza dough with oil, spread on the tomatoes, cover with cheese, and season with salt, pepper, and oregano. Let rise for another 15 minutes.

4 Put the dough on a floured work top and knead it for 5 minutes. Roll out the dough into a large round shape. Place on the baking sheet and leave in a warm place to rise, while you prepare the topping.

6 Bake in the oven for 20 minutes. Cut into slices and serve hot or cold.

Always be careful with a hot oven. Ask an adult to help you.

Glossary

Alps   A range of high mountains in Europe. The Alps spread through southeastern France, Switzerland, northern Italy, and Austria.

Buffalo   A large animal, related to cattle, with curved horns.

Cereal   Any of several different plants grown for their seeds, which can be used for food. For example, wheat, oats, and barley are cereals.

Croissants   Flaky bread rolls that are eaten for breakfast. They are crescent-shaped (like a new moon).

Diabetes   A health problem. People with diabetes have difficulty breaking down sugar in their bodies.

Diet   The kind of food a person generally eats.

Dough   A sticky paste made from flour and kneaded until it is very elastic. Bread is made from dough.

Game   Any wild animals that are hunted for sport.

Grazing land   Fields of grass where animals such as cattle and sheep are left to feed.

Imported   Brought in from another country.

Knead   To pound a mixture into a paste by working out the air with the palm of the hand.

Middle Ages   A period in Europe from about A.D. 1000 to the fifteenth century.

Midnight Mass   Mass is a church service held by Roman Catholics to remember Jesus Christ's Last Supper before he was put to death. Midnight Mass is a special service held at midnight on Christmas Eve.

Olive groves   Small areas planted with olive trees.

Paprika   A powder made from dried red peppers and used to flavor food.

Polluted   Made very dirty. Polluted land and water can be harmful to people, plants, and animals.

Preserving   Treating food so that it can be kept for a long time without going bad.

Risotto   An Italian rice dish.

Roman Catholics   Members of the Roman Catholic Church – a branch of the Christian Church – which is headed by the Pope in Rome.

Saffron   A bright yellow-colored spice made from crocus flowers.

Salami   Very spicy sausage.
Savory   Salty or spicy; not sweet.
Seasoning   Salt, pepper, and other flavorings used to make food tastier.
Songbirds   Small wild birds, such as blackbirds and thrushes, that are known for their calls. Some Italians trap songbirds to eat.
Spices   Strong-tasting substances that are used to flavor food (for example, ginger and nutmeg). They are often ground into powders.
Squid   An animal found in the sea with a long hollow body and tentacles. The body can be cut into rings and cooked.

Starchy   Containing starch. Starch is a kind of sugar found in certain foods, such as potatoes and rice.
Traditional   Made according to traditions, or customs, that have been passed down over the years, from one generation to another.
Vineyards   Fields where grapes for making into wine are grown.
Whey   A watery liquid that is left over when milk is clotted to make cheese.
Whole-wheat   Made from the whole of a grain or seed, including the outside husk. The complete wheat kernels are ground up to make whole-wheat flour.

Books to read

*Better Homes and Gardens New Junior Cookbook.*Des Moines: Meredith Corp., 1989.

Gaspari, Claudia. *Food in Italy.* Vero Beach, FL: Rourke Corp., 1989.

Martino, Theresa. *Pizza!.* Austin: Raintree Steck-Vaughn, 1989.

Robson, Denny A. *Cooking: Hands-On Projects.* Rainy Days. New York: Gloucester Press, 1991.

Sansone, Emma. *Getting to Know: Italy and Italian.* Getting to Know. Hauppauge, NY: Barron's Educational Series, 1993.

Wilkes, Angela. *My First Cookbook.* New York: Alfred A. Knopf , 1989.

Picture acknowledgments

The publishers would like to thank the following for allowing their photographs to be reproduced: Anthony Blake Photo Library 8 bottom, 22 left, 23, 26 bottom, 29 bottom, 32, 38; Cephas 6 right (M. Rock), 10 both (M. Rock), 12 (R. Beatty), 20, 21 top, 24 (M. Rock), 25 bottom (M. Rock), 26 top, 28 both (M. Rock); E. T. Archive 8 top; Eye Ubiquitous 11, 14 top, 30 (all P. Seheult); Hutchison Library 19, 22 right; Isabel Lilley 13 top, 35; Tony Stone Worldwide *cover* (main picture), 4 bottom, 6 left (J. Cornish), 7 bottom (N. DeVore), 37 (J. Jackson); Topham 9, 17 bottom, 40; Wayland Picture Library *cover* (inset picture), *frontispiece*, 13 bottom, 21 bottom, 43, 25 top; Zefa 4 top, 7 top, 14 bottom, 16, 17 top, 18, 27 top, 27 bottom, 29 top (W. Mahl), 31 (R. Bond), 34, 42.

The map artwork on page 5 was supplied by Peter Bull. The recipe artwork on pages 18-19 and 32-44 was supplied by Judy Stevens.

Index

Alps, the 4
Americas, the 10-11

bread 6, 13, 15, 26, 31
buffalo 22

cafes 12
cheese 6, 7, 22-23
Christmas food 30-31
coffee 12, 29
cooking equipment 14-15
corn 6, 10-11

diet 15

Easter food 31

farming 4-7
festivals 30-31
fish 15, 21, 34
fruit 6, 26-27

Gorgonzola 23
grapes 4, 28

ham 6, 20, 36-37
health 15
herbs 26

ices 12, 27, 40-41
Italy
    climate in 7
    geography of 4
    map of 5
    population of 4

markets 14
meat 20-21

Mediterranean Sea 4, 21
minestrone 32-33
mozzarella 23, 42

olives 4, 6-7, 24

panettone 30-31
Parmesan 22
pasta 6, 16-19, 32, 36-37
peppers 7, 10, 26
pizza 23, 42-44
Po River 25
polenta 11

rice 6, 25, 38-39
risotto 9, 38-39
Romans, ancient 8-9, 22, 26,
    27, 42
Rome 4

salami 6, 21
salt 9
Sardinia 4, 8
Sicily 4, 27
spices 9
stores 14

tomatoes 7, 10, 26, 42
torrone 31

vegetables 7, 10-11, 26-27

wheat 4, 6, 17
wines 6, 28-29